Table of Contents

The Wonder of Animals

By Kathleen N. Daly

Pictures by
Tim and Greg Hildebrandt

Golden Press • New York

Western Publishing Company, Inc.
Racine, Wisconsin

6

Unusual Animals

PLATYPUS

Animals come in all shapes and sizes, each one special in its own way. The most unusual of all animals is the little platypus, which is sometimes called the duckbill.

The platypus is a mammal, but it lays eggs like a bird. The mother platypus feeds her baby with milk from her body, but she has no nipples. Instead, the baby licks the milk from the mother's skin.

The platypus lives in a burrow deep under the ground near a stream. It swims underwater to catch worms and shrimp. It shovels these into its mouth with its bill, which is like a duck's.

The feet of the platypus are webbed like those of a duck, and its tail is shaped like a beaver's.

The platypus enters its tunnel-like home from the water. Then it goes uphill to the main room. There the mother platypus lays one or two or three eggs.

CHEETAH

The skinny, long-legged cheetah, with the beautiful spotted coat, is a cat. The cheetah is not as big as the lions and tigers, but it is the fastest moving of all land animals.

Cheetahs live on the African plains, where they hunt swift-footed antelopes and gazelles by running them down. Their sharp claws are always uncovered, like a dog's. (All other cats can pull in their claws.)

The cheetah can run 70 miles an hour for short distances. This is about twice as fast as a race horse can go.

SLOTH

The shaggy sloth is the slowest-moving
creature on earth. In fact it hardly moves at
all. It hangs upside down in a tree, eating
leaves and fruits. The only time it comes down
to earth is to move to another tree.

Some sloths have three toes on their front
feet. Others have only two.

A two-toed sloth. The three-toed sloth is
a bit bigger and a bit lighter in color.

HUMMINGBIRD

The tiniest of all birds is the hummingbird. Princess Helena's hummingbird is the smallest, for it is less than three inches long. A hummingbird's nest is like half a walnut shell, and the eggs are no bigger than peas.

A ruby-throated hummingbird

These beautiful little creatures feed on insects and the nectar from flowers. The hummingbird's long beak and coiled tongue can go deep inside a flower.

A hummingbird moves its wings so fast that they hum. These tiny creatures can stay still in the air, and can move backward, forward, or sideways, like helicopters.

Their feathers are so beautiful that people often compare them to jewels. They may also have long tails, or crests, or ruffs.

COWBIRD

Most birds build their own nests and look after their eggs until they hatch. Then both parents feed their babies until they are ready to fly away.

But the cowbird lays her eggs in the nest of another bird. When the cowbird hatches, it pushes the other eggs from the nest. And so the parents spend all their time feeding one large cowbird instead of a nestful of their own babies.

Yellowthroats feed a baby cowbird which is so big that it fills their nest.

BABOON

Baboons live on the ground during the day,
but at night they sleep high up in the trees.
They have strong arms and legs and sharp
teeth, so they are ready to fight off enemies.

   Baboons live in big troops, hunting together
for food. The babies cling underneath their
mother. Later, they learn to ride on her back.
All the grownups in a troop help to look after
the young ones.

KANGAROO

Australia is the home of many unusual animals. Many of them have pockets, or pouches, in which they rear their tiny babies.

A kangaroo baby is only about the size of a bumblebee when it is born. It lives in its mother's pouch until its back legs have grown long and strong. A baby kangaroo is called a joey.

Kangaroos have very strong legs. They can make long hops and give fierce kicks.

Other animals that rear their babies in pouches are opossums, wallabies, wombats, and koalas.

KOALA

This sleepy looking animal spends all its time feeding on the leaves of the eucalyptus or gum tree. After the baby is big enough to leave its mother's pouch, it rides on her back.

These little creatures are often called koala bears, but they are not bears at all. The first toy teddy bears were copies of koalas.

ANTEATER

Everything about this shaggy beast is long. It has a long body (about four feet), a long, thick, hairy tail (about three feet), a very long, thin snout, and a long, skinny, sticky tongue.

With its long, curved claws it digs holes in ants' nests. Then out comes its sticky tongue to scoop up hundreds of ants for a meal.

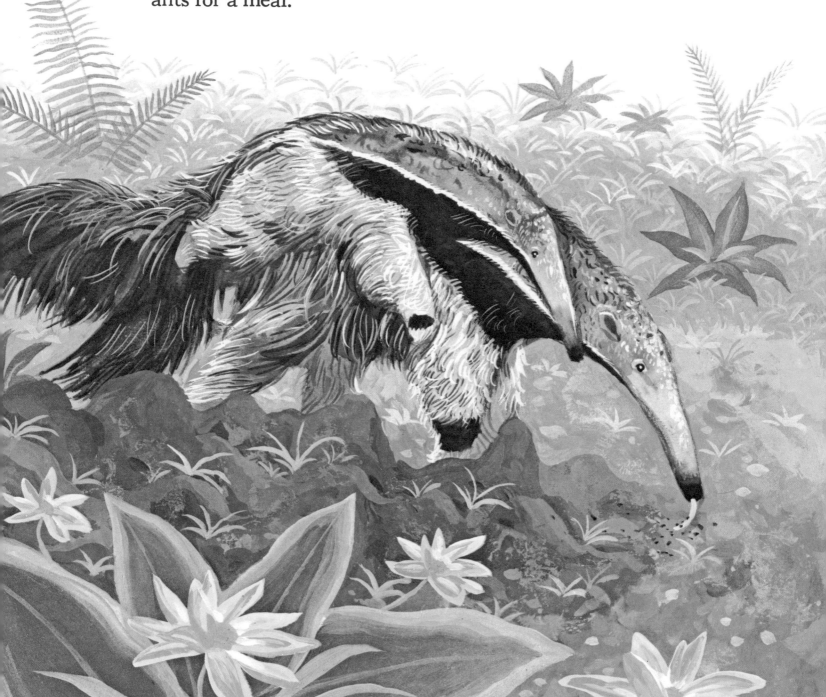

ECHIDNA

This little pincushion is often called the spiny anteater, but it is no relation to the true anteater. It does eat ants, though, and it has a long, sticky tongue for catching them.

Like many Australian animals, the echidna mother has a pouch. In it she places one egg. The egg hatches into a tiny echidna, which she carries in her pouch until it is about three inches long.

PEACOCK

Among birds, the male very often wears more colorful
feathers than the female. Males may have showy ruffs and
crests and tails. By far the most attractive tail among
animals is that of the peacock. The tail is about four feet
long and handsomely spotted with blue-green "eyes."
The peacock shows it off proudly in front of the plain
brown female, who is called a peahen.

   The peacock's voice is harsh and sounds like a rusty gate.
Peacocks may live to be very old.

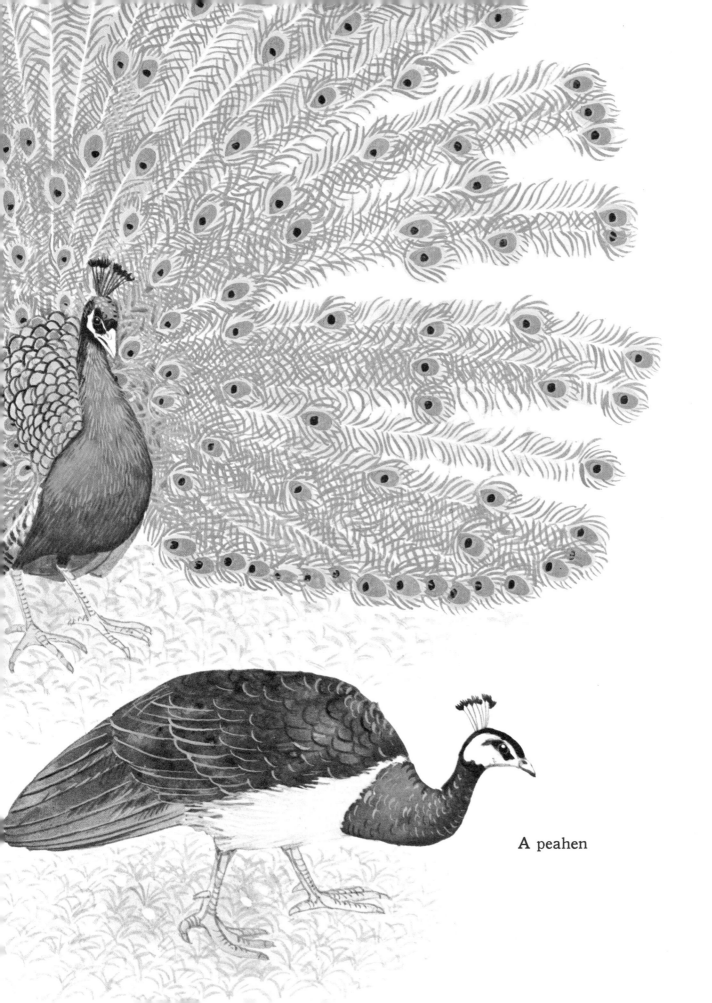

A peahen

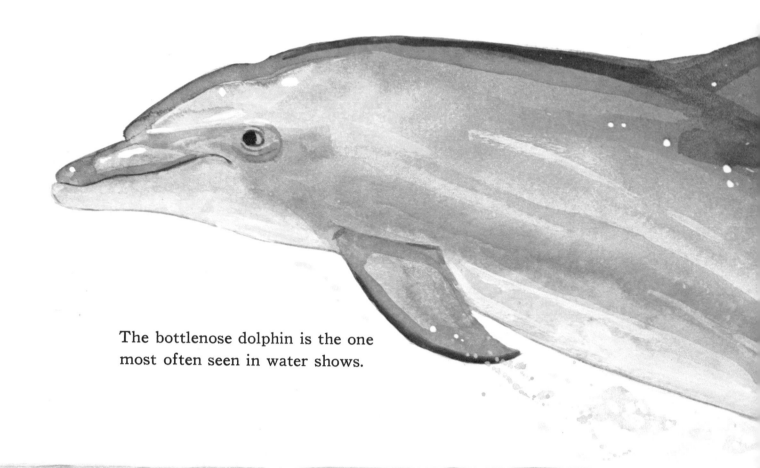

The bottlenose dolphin is the one most often seen in water shows.

DOLPHIN

Dolphins, which are often called porpoises, are small whales. They are mammals, not fish, and must put their heads above the water to breathe.

The most wonderful thing about these beautiful creatures is that they are very intelligent and playful. In aquariums they learn tricks very quickly, and seem to enjoy showing off. They talk to each other in grunts, squeaks, and whistles.

Dolphins travel together in friendly groups, and often follow ships, riding on the waves and leaping into the air. Female dolphins help each other to look after the baby dolphins.

PORTUGUESE MAN-OF-WAR

Many jellyfish are so tiny and transparent that they can hardly be seen. But the closely related Portuguese man-of-war can grow as big as a table and is brightly colored. Its long, stinging tentacles hang down to a depth of 40 feet. But this creature is not only one animal! It is made up of groups of animals that act as different parts of the body.

Nomeus fish, which are not hurt by the poison threads, swim along with the man-of-war, feeding on leftovers.

GIANT PANDA

The roly-poly, black-and-white giant panda looks like a walking toy, and many toys have been made to look like the giant panda. It is related to bears or to raccoons, but it comes from only one place in the world, a bamboo forest in China. There it eats nothing but bamboo shoots.

Baby pandas are very tiny (about five ounces) when they are born. Their mothers give them very good care.

There are two pandas in the zoo in Washington, D.C. These were given to the United States by the Republic of China.

DROMEDARY CAMEL

This member of the camel family can live
in the desert more easily than most other
animals. Its wide feet don't sink in the sand.
It can gallop swiftly and gracefully. It can
store fat in its hump, and so it doesn't need to
eat every day. Long eyelashes keep sand from
its eyes.

The dromedary never seems to get tired.
It is very useful to people who live in the
desert, for it can travel where no cars or even
horses can go. No wonder the dromedary is
called a "ship of the desert."

SEAHORSE

Most fish are fish-shaped, with streamlined bodies. But the
tiny seahorse has a head like a horse, and it swims upright.
It has a long tail it can use to hold on to seaweed.
Instead of scales, it has small bony plates all over its body.
This pretty little creature may be only two inches long.

   Most unusual of all is the way the father seahorse takes care
of the babies. He hatches the eggs in a pouch on his body.
Then, as the baby seahorses come out, the father keeps an eye
on them until they are big enough to swim away.

BAT

Bats are flying mammals; they are not birds. Their bodies are covered with fur, not feathers. And they don't lay eggs. Their babies are born live, and a mother bat feeds them with milk from her body.

Bats live together in huge flocks, often in caves. They sleep all day, and go out at sunset to find insects. They don't need to see well in the dark, for they have a wonderful "radar" system. This bounces sounds back to their sensitive ears and lets them know when they are about to fly into something like a house or a tree.

When the mother bat goes out, she leaves her baby hanging upside down to wait for her. Sometimes she may carry a tiny baby along with her.

The little brown bat helps farmers by eating insects.

Dinosaurs

RULERS OF THE LAND

Millions of years ago, our earth was the home of the dinosaurs. Among them were the biggest land animals that ever existed.

These huge creatures ruled the earth for a very long time. Then they disappeared, but nobody knows why. Only their bones and footprints, and some very old eggs, are left to tell us about them.

Scientists have put together dinosaur bones so we can see what those giant animals looked like.

When dinosaur bones were first found, people thought they belonged to giant lizards. The word "dinosaur" means "terrible lizard," and the largest of these beasts must have indeed seemed terrible to smaller animals.

DINOSAURS THAT WALKED ON TWO LEGS

Some of the first dinosaurs were only about as big as a small dog. Over many, many years they grew bigger and bigger. As they grew, their looks and habits changed, too.

Dinosaurs that walked on two legs were able to move faster than those that walked on four legs. After a long time there were many dinosaurs with short front legs. They used them like arms, to grab food.

Some dinosaurs were meat-eaters. They attacked and ate other dinosaurs. ORNITHOLESTES (or'ni'tho'LES'-teez) was a meat-eater. This miniature dinosaur had a long, whiplike tail and grasping fingers. Its name means "bird stealer," and that's just what Ornitholestes was.

PLATEOSAURUS (plat'e'o'SORE'us) was the biggest
of the early dinosaurs. It was about 20 feet long,
with a small head and a whiplike tail. It ate only
plants, but smaller dinosaurs stayed out of the way of
this tall, swift-moving animal.

THE AGE OF GIANTS

BRACHIOSAURUS (brack´e´o´SORE´us), of the mighty arms and legs, was the largest dinosaur of all. It was more than 80 feet long and stood 40 feet tall. That's about as long as three city buses and as high as a four-story building. And Brachiosaurus weighed 100,000 pounds! Other creatures were lucky it ate only plants.

On land, this gentle giant was too heavy to run fast and escape from the meat-eaters. It spent most of its time in lakes. There the water held up its body and made it seem lighter.

Brachiosaurus' ear-shaped nostrils were at the top of its head so that it could breathe when most of its body was under water.

BRONTOSAURUS (bron´toe´SORE´us) was a giant among giants. Its name means "thunder lizard," and its footsteps must have sounded like thunder when it walked the earth. It was about 70 feet long and weighed more than 60,000 pounds.

Because this gentle plant-eater was so heavy, it hardly ever left the water. When it had to come to shore to lay its eggs, it often was attacked by the fierce Allosaurus.

ALLOSAURUS (al'lo'SORE'us), a meat-eating
dinosaur, had strong claws and terrible teeth.
It was only 35 feet long, but it could fight the
giant Brontosaurus that was twice its size.

DIPLODOCUS (dip′LOD′o′cus) was almost 90 feet long, and longer than any other dinosaur. But it was not as heavy as Brachiosaurus or Brontosaurus. It had a long, thin neck and a long, thin tail that it used like a whip.

When Diplodocus searched for food in the water, its neck looked like a sea serpent rising from the deep. Its teeth were not very strong, and it could take only small bites. So Diplodocus had to spend most of its time eating so as to get enough food for its huge body.

OVIRAPTOR (o'vee'RAP'tor) was a small
dinosaur that liked to eat the eggs of other
dinosaurs. Its name means "egg stealer."

THE NEW DINOSAURS

After a while, the really giant dinosaurs disappeared from the earth. Maybe it was because they needed to eat a great many plants to stay alive, and there just weren't enough to go around. Anyway, the giant dinosaurs died out. Along with them went many of the meat-eaters that needed those giant plant-eaters for food.

New kinds of dinosaurs came along. They were smaller and they couldn't move fast. But they were protected by tough, spiked coats of armor.

STEGOSAURUS (steg'o'SORE'us) had large, bony plates down its back and a thick tail that ended in sharp spikes. Stegosaurus was about 20 feet long, but its brain was only as big as a walnut.

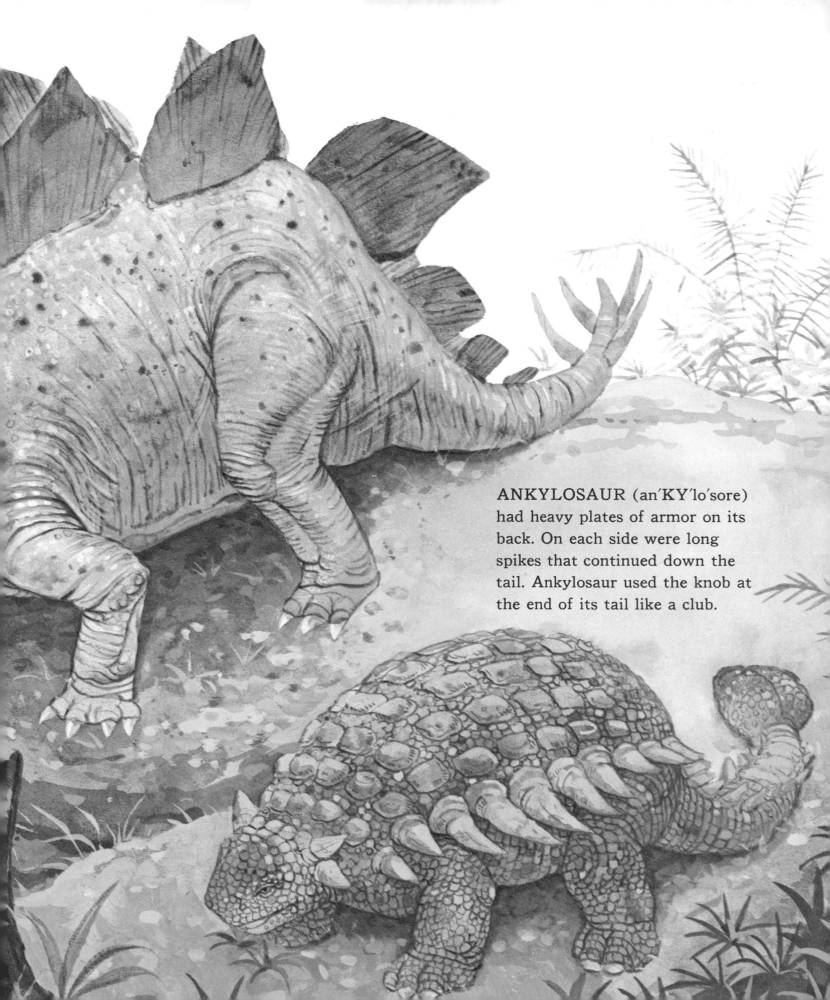

ANKYLOSAUR (an'KY'lo'sore) had heavy plates of armor on its back. On each side were long spikes that continued down the tail. Ankylosaur used the knob at the end of its tail like a club.

GORGOSAURUS (gor′go′SORE′us) was a fierce meat-eating dinosaur that stood nearly 40 feet tall. It was a swift two-legged runner with long, powerful legs. The terrible jaws of Gorgosaurus were filled with sharp, dagger-like teeth that it used to grab and tear its food.

PROTOCERATOPS (pro'toe'SER'o'tops)
was a plant-eater that was only about six
feet long. It was often attacked by the big
meat-eaters. But Protoceratops was
protected by armor and a tough, bony frill
at the back of its head. It always put up
a good fight.

Another animal that lived in the
days of the dinosaur was the
RHAMPHORHYNCHUS (ram'
fo'RINK'us). It flew, but it was
a reptile, and not a bird. The
leathery skin that stretched
between its body and its arms
became its wings.

DUCKBILLS

Some dinosaurs lived along the shores of swamps. They had strange feet that were webbed like a duck's. With these huge feet, they could walk in the soft mud along the water's edge without sinking in.

Such dinosaurs were called duckbills. Their heads were shaped something like a duck's, too.

TRACHODON (TRACK'o'don) was about 30 feet long. Its name means "rough tooth," and Trachodon had about 2,000 teeth in its duck-billed mouth.

IGUANODON (i′GWAN′o′don), or "lizard tooth," was smaller than Trachodon and had hands shaped like human hands. The thumb was a spiked claw. Iguanodon usually walked on two legs, balancing on its webbed feet and tail.

HORNED DINOSAURS

Many dinosaurs had horns on their heads and looked a little like large, fierce rhinoceroses. But these horned dinosaurs were peaceful plant-eaters. Their horns protected them from the sharp claws and powerful teeth of the meat-eaters.

STYRACOSAURUS (sty'rack'o'SORE'us), or "spike lizard," had a crown of six long horns on its head and another horn tilted up from its nose.

TRICERATOPS (try'SER'a'tops) was like an armored tank, with a long, bony collar and three sharp horns. This eight-ton plant-eater was about six feet tall and was feared by even the giant killer-dinosaurs.

TYRANNOSAURUS (tie′ ran′o′SORE′us) REX was the most terrible dinosaur that ever lived. This giant meat-eater was nearly 60 feet long and as tall as a two-story house.

Tyrannosaurus was a fierce hunter, and other dinosaurs feared its powerful jaws and long, sharp teeth. It was a "terrible lizard" indeed, and one of the last of the great dinosaurs.

PTERANODON (ter'AN'o'don) was a large flying reptile. It had a wingspread of over 20 feet.

49

Hide and Defend

WINTER COATS

For wild animals, each day is a game of hide-and-seek. But it's a dangerous and serious game.

The danger comes when animals leave their nests and burrows and go to look for food. As they move about, they try not to be eaten by other creatures.

Animals have many ways of hiding and of defending themselves. Sometimes the color of their coats helps them to hide.

All the creatures on this page have brown fur or feathers during the short summer of the Arctic, where they live.

weasel

ptarmigan

collared lemming

Arctic fox

snowshoe hare

In the winter, fox and ermine, ptarmigan, snowshoe hare and collared lemming are white as the snow around them. Their brown coats and feathers have slowly changed with the seasons. It is hard to see their new white coats against the snow.

Arctic fox

snowshoe hare

ermine

ptarmigan

collared lemming

The polar bear, huge and fearsome, is white all year round, and he seldom leaves the snowy white ice floes of the Far North.

53

STRIPES AND SPOTS

Which zebras are harder to see—
zebras in the jungle
or zebras in the zoo?

In a zoo, the black-and-white striped zebra stands out gaily from its background. But in its natural home the stripes blend well with the brilliant light and deep shadows of the trees and tall grasses.

The stripes also help to break up the shape of the zebra. From a distance it is hard to tell where the animal's head is, or its legs.

Many deer, antelope, and gazelles have spots and stripes, especially when they are young. These make it easier for the little animals to hide.

This baby deer, called a fawn, has white spots on its coat. When danger is near, it stays very still. The light and shade on its coat make it hard to see. Another thing that helps is that the fawn has no smell! And so the enemy cannot see it or smell it, and usually passes it by.

There are other animals that are hard to see in the jungle. The spots of the leopard and the stripes of the orange-and-black tiger help these animals to fade into the background of the trees and dry grass.

leopard

SPEED HELPS, TOO

There are many kinds of antelope. Their delicate stripes blend well with the dappled light and shade of their homes.

Another protection of these animals is their speed. The pronghorn antelope can run 60 miles an hour, over short distances.

tiger

The eland is the biggest member of the antelope family.

WHICH IS WHICH?

There are many millions of insects in the world, far more than there are people. Yet we don't see them very often, for insects have many ways of hiding.

For example, many insects are colored green or brown, like the plants among which they live.

This butterfly, the kallima, looks like a dead leaf.

The inchworm can hold itself so stiffly that it looks just like a twig.

The glass-winged butterfly has see-through wings.

The walking stick looks like a stick—until it moves.

When some moths come to rest on a tree, their markings line up with the markings on the bark.

Here's something surprising! There are harmless insects that look like dangerous ones!

The gentle bee-fly looks like the stinging bumblebee.

The viceroy butterfly is avoided by birds, because it looks like the bad-tasting monarch butterfly.

The porcupine fish can blow itself up into a big ball that is hard to swallow.

The sargassum fish is not easy to spot. Its knobs, tassels, frills, and streamers look exactly like the seaweeds of the Sargasso Sea, where it lives.

HIDING IN THE SEA

Ocean creatures, too, must protect themselves from other animals. They have many tricks that can fool even the most watchful hunters.

The flounder changes its speckles to match the sand or gravel of the sea bottom where it is resting.

The sponge crab cuts out a piece of sponge (which no fish will eat) and holds it over its back.

People think of octopuses and squids as great monsters of the deep. But many of them are small and very shy. They hide their soft bodies in underwater caves.

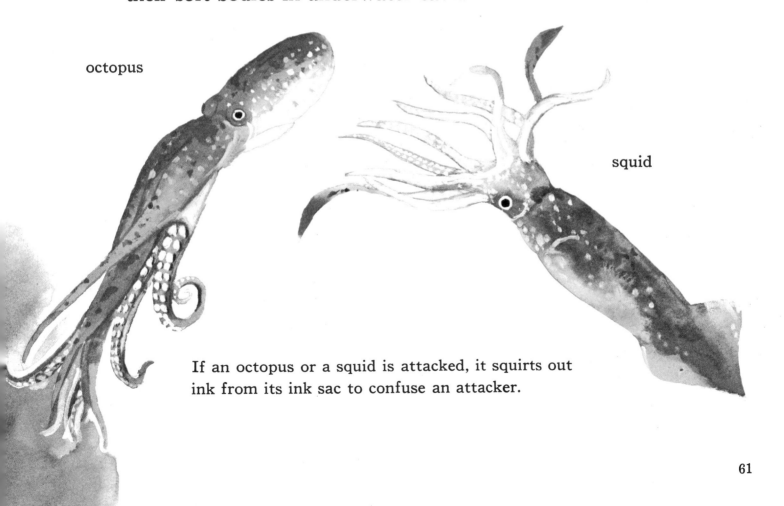

octopus

squid

If an octopus or a squid is attacked, it squirts out ink from its ink sac to confuse an attacker.

ANIMALS THAT PLAY DEAD

Some animals, instead of running or hiding, "play possum" as the opossum does. This little animal is unusual in many ways. It rears its tiny babies in a pouch, like a kangaroo. When the babies are older, the mother carries them on her back.

When the opossum is attacked, it lies very still. Its enemy may think it is dead and leave it alone.

Some snakes and small animals "hide" by being very, very still. For example, rabbits, mice, and other small animals often sit quietly and do not move when danger is near.

The hog-nosed snake is another animal that plays dead. First, it puts on a very good show of being in pain. It twists and turns its long body as if it were hurt. Then it rolls over and lies still as if it had died.

A rabbit "freezing"

Some lizards pant, blow themselves up, and do little push-ups.

Other lizards show off their frilly collars and the crests on their backs, which makes them look big and scary.

Many lizards, when caught by their tail, can snap it off and then grow a new one.

Some lizards can change color.

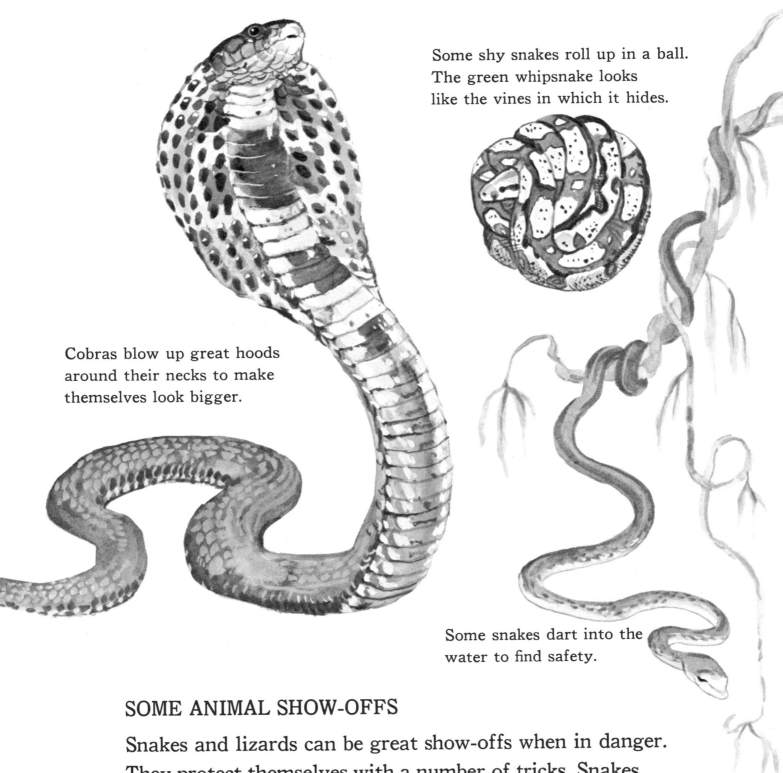

Some shy snakes roll up in a ball.
The green whipsnake looks
like the vines in which it hides.

Cobras blow up great hoods
around their necks to make
themselves look bigger.

Some snakes dart into the
water to find safety.

SOME ANIMAL SHOW-OFFS

Snakes and lizards can be great show-offs when in danger.
They protect themselves with a number of tricks. Snakes
have especially clever ways of defending themselves.
Most of them hiss and sometimes spit.

ANIMALS IN ARMOR

Some animals, such as the turtle, have sturdy suits of armor. The turtle moves so slowly on its short legs that hunters can easily catch up with it. But then it pulls its head and legs into its shell, and there it hides.

The turtle's shell has a bottom and a top part. Even a sharp knife or a bear's strength can't pry that shell open. So the turtle is usually safe inside.

A turtle walking in the woods

The turtle safely inside its shell

The snail, too, has a shell on its back. It can pull its soft body into the shell and stay there, safe and snug.

Some armadillos have a jointed coat of armor. This one can roll itself into a tight ball so that nothing can get at its soft underbelly.

The pangolin, too, can roll into a ball. Its scales are very hard and sharp and can give bad cuts. That is why most animals leave it alone with its meal of ants.

HOW TO KEEP OTHERS AWAY

The skunk leads a peaceful life, for its neighbors seem to know about its scent spray. The skunk's striking black-and-white coat says, "Watch out!" If its attacker doesn't go away, the skunk turns its back and lifts its tail. Then out comes the spray, which stings the eyes and leaves a very bad smell.

A mother skunk with her babies. She protects the babies with a nasty-smelling spray.

Some other little animals use
their prickly coats to keep
strangers away.

Long, sharp spines on most of the porcupine's body
keep the animal safe. If the prickles stick into a soft
nose or mouth, they are hard to get out.

Another prickly animal is the little hedgehog.
It rolls itself into a ball, and most animals will
leave it alone.

SOME BIRD TRICKS

Birds are the most brilliantly colored creatures in nature. Often they live together in large flocks and help look after each other. Also, they move so fast that their enemies cannot catch them.

But a nesting bird must hide. Nearly always, the mother bird and her babies are speckled and dull in color. This makes them hard to spot.

If a hunter comes near the nest of a plover, the mother bird drags herself away as if she were wounded. She leads the enemy away from the nest.

The bittern, standing in the reeds, can look exactly like a cattail. The bird stretches its neck and sways in the breeze.

Today's Biggest Animals

BLUE WHALE

The blue whale is the biggest animal in the world. It is even bigger than any dinosaur that ever lived. It may weigh 150 tons and be more than 100 feet long.

This giant whale lives in the ocean. But it is a mammal, not a fish. Like all mammals, the mother whale feeds her baby with milk from her body. The baby calf is about 25 feet long when it is born. The mother swims under the newborn baby to raise its head above water so it can breathe.

Whales breathe air, just as we do. They have to come to the surface to do this. When the whale breathes out through the blowholes at the top of its head, the moist air forms a fountain of spray.

ELEPHANT

The biggest land animal is the African elephant. A large male weighs more than 12,000 pounds and is more than 10 feet tall. (The Indian elephant is smaller, with shorter tusks.)

In Africa, elephants travel in herds, searching for food. They use their trunks to reach high into trees for leaves and twigs. They use their tusks to dig for roots in the ground.

At the waterhole, elephants cool off by filling their trunks with water and showering themselves.

Baby elephants travel with the herd when they are only a few days old. The mothers and the other grownups protect the babies from danger.

Sometimes the hippo baby rides on its mother's back in the water.

HIPPOPOTAMUS

Next to the elephant, the hippopotamus is the biggest animal. Its name means "river horse." This bulky beast is 14 feet long and weighs up to 8,000 pounds.

In the warm, muddy rivers where they live, hippos are graceful swimmers. They spend most of the day in the water because the sun is too hot for their tender skins. At night, they leave the river to feed on tall grasses.

Often a hippo just stands in the water with only its nose and puffy little eyes showing. It has a very sleepy look. When a hippo gives a big yawn, its huge pink mouth opens like a door.

RHINOCEROS

There are different kinds of rhinoceroses. Some have one horn. Some have two horns. Some are not as big as others, or are a different color. The biggest rhinos weigh up to 7,000 pounds and are more than five feet tall.

One kind of rhino has a leathery skin with thick, armorlike plates. It looks like an armored tank as it lumbers across the prairie.

With its bulky body and short legs, the rhino doesn't look as if it could run very fast. But it can. If it hears a strange sound or picks up a strange smell, it will often lower its head and charge. When a big rhino charges, the earth trembles.

GIRAFFE

The tallest of all animals is the giraffe. Some giraffes are more than 18 feet tall. Even newborn baby giraffes are as tall as a man.

With such a long neck, it is easy for a giraffe to feed on leaves and twigs high in the treetops. But when a giraffe is thirsty its long neck can be a problem. It has to spread its front legs far apart to lower its head to the water.

Giraffes have big, velvety eyes shaded by thick lashes. Because they are so tall, they can see much farther than other animals and can give warning of danger.

KODIAK BEAR

When the big, brown Kodiak bear stands up, it is nearly 11 feet tall. It weighs a lot, too—about 1,500 pounds. It has huge feet and long, dangerous claws. The Kodiak is the biggest bear, bigger even than the giant grizzly.

In the winter, two tiny bear cubs are born in a cave. They stay in the cave until spring comes. Then their mother teaches them where to find honey and berries, and how to catch fish. When winter comes again, the bears return to the cave, where they sleep away the long, cold months.

The Kodiak gets its name from the island off the Alaskan coast where it lives.

MOOSE

Another great animal of the northern forests is the moose. It is the largest member of the deer family.

The male moose grows horns, called antlers. Each year these grow bigger. Sometimes they are more than six feet across and may weigh over 100 pounds. The huge antlers are shed every winter but grow back in the summer.

A big moose is seven feet high at the shoulder and may weigh up to 1,800 pounds. When he comes crashing through the forest, the other animals take cover.

TIGER

The tiger, with its handsome striped coat, is one of the most beautiful of all animals. When it moves through the tall, waving grasslands, its stripes keep it almost hidden.

Tigers rest during the day and hunt in the evening shadows. Even though they weigh 500 pounds, these big animals make hardly a sound as they creep up on their prey. They are patient hunters. They will even swim across rivers in search of food.

Most tigers are about the same size as lions. But the male Siberian tiger may be bigger than any lion. It lives in the far North, where winters are cold and snowy. Few people have seen this biggest of cats, for it is very rare.

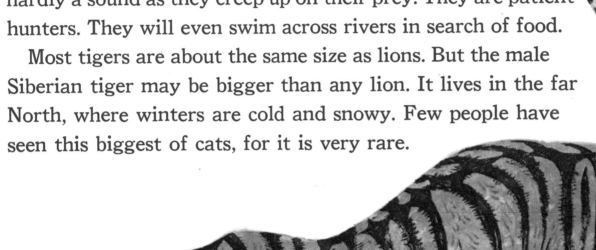

LION

Lions are the only big cats that live together in family groups. These families are called "prides," and sometimes there are as many as 20 lions in one pride. The spotted cubs play together like kittens, while the fathers nap in the heat of the day and the mothers keep a sharp lookout.

When the cubs are old enough, their mothers take them along on hunting trips. The cubs learn how to hide in the tall grass and how to run and pounce like mighty hunters.

OSTRICH

The eight-foot-tall ostrich is the biggest bird in the world. This strange-looking creature has a small head, a long, bare neck, and long, bare legs. Beautiful feathers cover the rest of its body. The ostrich cannot fly, but it can run very fast on its powerful legs. Its legs can also kick out dangerously at enemies.

Ostrich eggs are about the size of a child's football. Out of them hatch chicks with spiky feathers. The babies grow about one foot a month and are soon as tall as their parents.

CONDOR

One of the biggest of all flying birds is the condor. When its wings are spread in flight they are nearly 10 feet across. These birds live in the mountains, where they glide on air currents, searching for small animals far below.

TRUMPETER SWAN

The trumpeter swan is one of the largest water birds. This graceful swan "trumpets" a loud call that can be heard for miles.

KOMODO DRAGON

Many lizards are small and good to have around because they catch lots of insects. But the lizard that lives on Komodo Island is big enough to be scary. It is 10 feet long and weighs more than 300 pounds. A lash of its heavy tail can knock over even a large animal.

The Komodo dragon prowls the island, hunting for deer to eat. When it finds one, the terrible dragon attacks it, biting down hard with razor-sharp teeth and slashing with its long claws.

CROCODILE

The biggest crocodiles are more than 20 feet long. Like all reptiles, they spend most of their time basking in the warm sun or finding a shady spot in which to cool off. In a river, they often lie just below the water. They look like floating logs, except for their watchful eyes.

The great, smiling jaws of a crocodile are full of sharp teeth, and its powerful tail is used like a whip. Other animals stay away when this hungry reptile is looking for a meal.

Young crocodiles hatch from eggs. For the first few days the babies follow their mother around,
but then they go off on their own.

ALLIGATOR

Alligators are not as big as crocodiles, but they are pretty big just the same. They look a lot like crocodiles. But when an alligator's mouth is closed, none of its teeth show. That's one way to tell the two reptiles apart. Also, an alligator's head is shorter and thicker than a crocodile's.

ELEPHANT SEAL

The elephant seal gets its name from its droopy nose that reminds people of an elephant's trunk. Male elephant seals are much bigger than the females. A big male is more than 20 feet long and weighs 5,000 pounds.

Hundreds of elephant seals gather on rocky beaches in spring, when their babies are born. The father seals protect the nurseries, snorting loudly through their "trunks" to keep other animals away.

Baby seals are called pups. They are born with black, woolly coats. When the babies are old enough, their mothers teach them to swim.

LEATHERBACK SEA TURTLE

Most turtles have hard, bony shells. But not the leatherback sea turtle. Its shell is covered with tough leather plates.

This monster of the seas can weigh up to 2,000 pounds and is about nine feet long. The mother turtle only comes ashore when it is time to lay her eggs. She digs a hole in the sand, leaves the eggs, and returns to the sea.

The baby leatherbacks seem to know that their home is in the sea, and they hurry across the sand to reach it as soon as they hatch. The tiny babies are good swimmers, using their fat little flippers to push them through the water.

GORILLA

Gorillas are the biggest apes. They weigh as much as
450 pounds. But when a baby gorilla is born it weighs about
four pounds. (A human baby weighs about seven pounds.)
The mother gorilla takes good care of her baby and carries
it everywhere with her. When the baby is older, it likes to ride
around on its mother's back.

Gorillas live in family groups. They travel most of the day,
looking for fruits and plants to eat. At night, they make
large, leafy nests in trees and sleep late into the morning.

ANACONDA

The anaconda is the biggest and heaviest snake in the world. When it stretches out to its full size, it may be over 30 feet long, and may weigh 600 pounds.

This giant snake lives in swamps. In the daytime, it usually lies in the water, with only its eyes showing. At night, it hunts for a bird or other small animal. When it finds one, it coils its great body around the victim and crushes it.

KING COBRA

Some snakes kill their prey by biting them with their poisonous fangs. The biggest of these poisonous snakes is the king cobra. It mostly eats other snakes.

Just before the cobra attacks, its head swells up to many times its normal size. It looks very, very fierce.

WHALE SHARK

There are many big fish in the sea. But the biggest of them all is the whale shark. It may be 60 feet long and weigh about 30,000 pounds. It is even bigger than many whales.

The whale shark has a huge mouth. Two big people could fit inside it. And it has 3,600 or more teeth! But this giant of the seas does not attack people. It eats only tiny fish and plants. Of course, such a big shark needs to eat thousands of little fish each day.

DEVILFISH

The devilfish is another ocean giant. It measures
20 feet across and looks as if it has great flat wings.
It flaps these "wings" as it swims, and sometimes
leaps high out of the water.